conte

British & North American Readers:
Please note that Australian cup and
spoon measurements are metric. A quick
conversion guide appears on page 63.
A glossary explaining unfamiliar terms
and ingredients begins on page 60.

2 fast food tips

There's no reason why tasty, nutritious food can't also be speedy to prepare. These commonsense hints will help you deliver the meal to the table in record time!

stock up

Organise your weekly menu, then shop for it all at the one time. A well-stocked pantry, refrigerator and freezer ensure there's no need to waste time ducking out at the last minute for missing grocery items. Consider using the lists (right) for basic foods used in the recipes in this book. Remember, once jars and bottles have been opened, secure lids tightly and keep them refrigerated. Transfer leftover canned food to a non-reactive container.

half now, half later

Thinking ahead can save you plenty of time later, when you have none to spare. An ideal example: when appropriate, double the ingredient quantities of a recipe so that you can freeze half of the dish for another occasion. Soups, casseroles, stocks, cakes, biscuits, etc, are all well-suited to this suggestion.

Follow these freezing tips:
- Let cooked food, such as casseroles, stand, covered, at room temperature, 1 hour before placing in refrigerator to completely cool, then placing in the freezer. When using rigid containers, leave 2cm to 5cm space for expansion of the food when it freezes.
- Remove air from the package to be frozen so that food does not dry out, discolour or absorb other flavours.
- Label all packages and containers by content's name, date packaged, weight and portion size.
- The fastest way to defrost is in the microwave oven, but otherwise thaw food in refrigerator for 10 to 24 hours (depending on the quantity of food).

other time-savers
- Dried herbs can be used instead of fresh: 1 teaspoon of any dried herb is equivalent to 1 tablespoon of that herb, chopped and fresh.
- Buy pricier cuts of meat – they usually require no trimming, and lean meat cooks faster as well as tasting better.
- Some fantastically fast accompaniments to meals include instant polenta and couscous, to which you merely add boiling water. A perfect, easy way to fill out a stir-fry is with the addition of rice vermicelli noodles – preparation is a simple matter of pouring boiling water over the noodles in a bowl.
- Leftover cooked rice and pasta freezes beautifully, and can be reheated in a microwave oven.
- When time is of the essence, use bottled crushed garlic, minced ginger, chopped chillies and lemon grass, etc, in place of fresh ingredients.

pantry

black mustard seeds
breadcrumbs, stale
cajun seasoning
canned butter beans
canned cannellini beans
canned chickpeas
canned corn kernels
canned creamed corn
canned green peppercorns
canned potatoes
canned tomatoes
canned tuna
caraway seeds
chilli powder
chilli sauce (mild, sweet)
cinnamon sticks
coconut cream and milk
coriander, ground
cornflour
couscous
cumin, ground
curry pastes
curry powder
dried herbs (basil,
    mixed, thyme)
flour, plain
garam masala
ginger, ground
honey
lentils, red
mango chutney
mustard, seeded
noodles
nutmeg, ground
oil (olive, peanut,
    sesame, vegetable)
olives, black
pasta
rice (arborio, long-grain)
satay sauce
sesame seeds
soy sauce

stocks, powdered and
    in tetra packs
sugar (white, brown)
sun-dried tomatoes
sweet paprika
tabasco sauce
taco seasoning mix
tandoori paste
tomato paste
tomato sauce
turmeric, ground
vinegar (balsamic,
    cider, white wine)
wine, dry red

refrigerator

butter/margarine
cheese (cheddar, fetta,
    mozzarella, parmesan)
cream
eggs
milk
sour cream
yogurt

freezer

bacon
bread (pide, pitta)
nuts (peanuts, pine nuts)
pizza bases

fruit and vegetables

carrots
chillies
garlic
ginger
lemons
limes
onions
oranges
potatoes
pumpkin
tomatoes

4 lentil, pumpkin and
spinach curry

1 cup (200g)
red lentils

700g pumpkin, peeled,
chopped coarsely

1 tablespoon
peanut oil

1 medium white onion
(150g), sliced thinly

1 tablespoon grated
fresh ginger

2 cloves garlic,
crushed

$1/4$ cup (65g) mild
curry paste

1 tablespoon black
mustard seeds

$1^2/_3$ cups (400ml)
coconut cream

350g baby
spinach leaves

1 tablespoon coarsely
chopped fresh
coriander leaves

Cook lentils in large saucepan of boiling
water, uncovered, about 10 minutes or until
tender; drain.

Meanwhile, boil, steam or microwave pumpkin
until tender; drain.

Heat oil in wok or large frying pan; stir-fry onion,
ginger and garlic until onion is browned lightly.
Add paste and seeds; stir-fry until fragrant.
Add lentils, pumpkin and coconut cream; stir-fry
until sauce boils. Add spinach and coriander;
stir-fry, tossing until spinach is just wilted.

SERVES 4
Per serving 32.3g fat; 2138kJ

6 chicken cacciatore

2 tablespoons olive oil

8 (1.3kg) chicken thigh cutlets

2 cloves garlic, crushed

4 medium tomatoes (760g), peeled, seeded, sliced thinly

2 tablespoons brown sugar

1 tablespoon balsamic vinegar

¼ cup (30g) seeded black olives, sliced thinly

2 tablespoons finely shredded fresh basil leaves

Heat oil in large frying pan; cook chicken, in batches, until browned both sides and cooked through. Drain on absorbent paper; cover.
Add garlic to same pan; cook, stirring, until soft. Add tomato, sugar, vinegar and olives; cook, stirring, until sugar dissolves. Simmer, uncovered, about 5 minutes or until tomato sauce thickens. Serve chicken topped with tomato sauce, sprinkled with basil.

SERVES 4
Per serving 28.7g fat; 2932kJ

in garlic butter

400g flat mushrooms

2 tablespoons
peanut oil

1 large brown onion
(200g), sliced thinly

2 cloves garlic, crushed

400g Swiss brown
mushrooms

400g button
mushrooms

2 teaspoons garlic salt

100g butter

Quarter flat
mushrooms. Heat
oil in wok or large
frying pan; stir-fry
onion, garlic and
all mushrooms, in
batches, until tender.
Return mushrooms to
wok with garlic salt
and chopped butter;
stir-fry until butter
is melted. Serve on
toast, sprinkled with
baby basil leaves,
if desired.

SERVES 4
Per serving
30.6g fat; 1466kJ

8 turkish lamb with spinach and pine nuts

1 tablespoon olive oil

¹/₂ cup (80g) pine nuts

750g minced lamb

2 large brown onions (400g), chopped finely

2 cloves garlic, crushed

4 birdseye chillies, seeded, chopped finely

1 tablespoon ground coriander

1 tablespoon ground cumin

500g spinach, trimmed, chopped coarsely

¹/₄ cup finely chopped fresh mint leaves

4 large pitta breads

300ml yogurt

1 tablespoon lemon juice

Heat half of the oil in large frying pan; cook pine nuts, stirring, until browned lightly. Drain on absorbent paper.

Cook lamb in same pan, in batches, until browned.

Heat remaining oil in same pan; cook onion, garlic, chilli, coriander and cumin until onion is browned lightly. Return lamb to pan with nuts, spinach and mint; cook, stirring, until spinach is just wilted.

Divide lamb mixture among pitta; serve with combined yogurt and juice.

SERVES 4
Per serving 42.2g fat; 3431kJ

satay chicken burgers

1 long loaf
Turkish pide

750g minced chicken

1 cup (70g) stale
breadcrumbs

1/4 cup finely chopped
fresh coriander leaves

2/3 cup (160ml)
satay sauce

1 large carrot
(180g), peeled

1 Lebanese
cucumber (130g)

1 cup (250ml) yogurt

Quarter pide widthways; cut each piece in half horizontally. Place pieces, cut-side up, on oven tray; toast, on both sides, under heated grill, until browned lightly.

Combine chicken, breadcrumbs, coriander and half of the sauce in medium bowl; shape into four patties. Cook in large heated oiled frying pan until browned both sides and cooked through.

Meanwhile, using a vegetable peeler, slice carrot and cucumber into thin strips.

Top each of the pide bases with a burger, equal amounts of carrot and cucumber strips, and combined yogurt and remaining sauce.

SERVES 4
Per serving 25.2g fat; 3379kJ

pork and snake-beans
madras

4 bacon rashers, chopped coarsely

1 tablespoon peanut oil

700g pork fillets, sliced thinly

1 large white onion (200g), sliced thinly

1/4 cup (65g) Madras curry paste

200g snake beans, chopped coarsely

1/2 cup (125ml) beef stock

1 tablespoon tomato paste

In a dry heated wok or large frying pan, stir-fry bacon until crisp; drain on absorbent paper.

Heat oil in same wok; stir-fry pork and onion, in batches, until browned.

Stir-fry curry paste in same wok until just fragrant. Add snake beans to wok with pork mixture, bacon, stock and paste; stir-fry, tossing until sauce boils.

SERVES 4
Per serving 17.5g fat; 1642kJ

pork chops
valenciana

4 pork loin chops

1/2 cup (175g) orange marmalade

2 tablespoons mild chilli sauce

1 tablespoon cider vinegar

1 teaspoon grated fresh ginger

1 teaspoon ground cumin

3 green onions, sliced thinly

Cook pork, uncovered, in large heated oiled frying pan until browned both sides and cooked through. Remove pork from pan; cover to keep warm.
Meanwhile, cook marmalade, sauce, vinegar, ginger and cumin in small saucepan, stirring, until sauce thickens slightly; stir onion into sauce. Serve sauce over pork.

SERVES 4
Per serving
5.7g fat; 1167kJ

lemon ginger
fish fillets

4 (800g) firm white fish fillets

80g butter

1 teaspoon finely grated lemon rind

2 tablespoons lemon juice

1 teaspoon grated fresh ginger

2 tablespoons finely chopped fresh parsley

3 green onions, sliced thinly

Cook fish in large heated oiled frying pan until browned lightly both sides and cooked through. **Meanwhile**, melt butter in small saucepan; add rind, juice and ginger, cook 1 minute. Stir parsley and onion into butter sauce; serve sauce over fish.

SERVES 4
Per serving 20.8g fat; 1485kJ

lemon pepper
schnitzel

8 (720g) veal
schnitzels

300ml cream

1 teaspoon finely
grated lemon rind

2 tablespoons
lemon juice

2 teaspoons finely
chopped fresh
rosemary

1 teaspoon chicken
stock powder

1 teaspoon cracked
black pepper

Cook veal in large heated oiled frying pan, in batches, until
browned both sides and cooked as desired. Remove veal from
pan; cover to keep warm.

Add remaining ingredients to same pan. Bring to a boil; simmer,
uncovered, about 5 minutes or until sauce thickens slightly. Return
veal to pan; coat with sauce.

SERVES 4
Per serving 38.6g fat; 2383kJ

spiced veal cutlets
with coriander raita

1/4 cup (60ml) yogurt

1 teaspoon finely
grated lemon rind

1 tablespoon
lemon juice

1 tablespoon
tandoori paste

8 (1kg) veal cutlets

coriander raita

1 cup (250ml) yogurt

2 Lebanese cucumbers
(260g), seeded,
chopped finely

1 large tomato
(250g), seeded,
chopped finely

1 teaspoon
ground cumin

1 tablespoon
lemon juice

1 tablespoon finely
chopped fresh
coriander leaves

Combine yogurt, rind, juice, paste and veal
in large bowl, cover; stand 10 minutes.
Char-grill (or grill or barbecue) veal until
browned both sides and cooked as desired.
Serve veal with Coriander Raita.
Coriander Raita Combine ingredients in
medium bowl.

SERVES 4
Per serving 8.5g fat; 1252kJ

16 tuna with char-grilled vegetables

3 medium
potatoes (600g)

2 medium
lemons (280g)

2 pickled baby
dill cucumbers,
sliced thinly

4 small tuna
steaks (600g)

2 teaspoons drained
green peppercorns

2 teaspoons drained
tiny capers

Boil, steam or microwave potatoes until just tender; cut each potato into four slices. Cut each lemon into six slices. Cook lemon, potato and cucumber in batches, on heated oiled grill plate (or grill or barbecue) until browned and just tender; cover to keep warm.

Cook tuna on same grill plate until browned both sides and cooked as desired; cover to keep warm.

Heat peppercorns and capers on same grill plate until hot.

Divide potato among plates, then top with tuna, lemon and cucumber. Sprinkle with peppercorns and capers.

SERVES 4
Per serving 4.7g fat; 1212kJ

chicken and vegetable
burritos

1 tablespoon
vegetable oil

300g chicken thigh
fillets, sliced thinly

2 medium brown
onions (300g),
sliced thinly

2 teaspoons
ground cumin

2 teaspoons
ground coriander

1 teaspoon
sweet paprika

400g can tomatoes

2 small carrots (140g),
chopped finely

250g broccoli,
chopped finely

2 tablespoons
sour cream

4 flour tortillas

Heat oil in large frying pan; cook chicken, in batches, until browned and cooked through, drain on absorbent paper. Cook onion in same pan, stirring, until soft. Add cumin, coriander and paprika; cook, stirring, until fragrant. **Stir** in undrained crushed tomatoes and carrot; cook, stirring, until carrot is tender and sauce is thick. Return chicken to pan with broccoli; cook, stirring, until broccoli is just tender. Stir in cream. Divide mixture among tortillas, roll up. Serve with salad and grated cheddar cheese, if desired.

SERVES 4
Per serving 14.5g fat; 1191kJ

18 grilled lime and pepper
ocean trout

2 teaspoons finely grated
lime rind

½ teaspoon cracked
black pepper

2 tablespoons olive oil

2 tablespoons finely chopped
fresh chives

4 (720g) ocean trout cutlets

1 large red onion (300g)

2 medium limes (160g)

Combine rind, pepper, oil and
chives in large bowl; add fish, turn
to coat in mixture.
Cut onion and limes into wedges.
Char-grill (or grill or barbecue) fish,
onion and lime, until onion and lime
are browned and fish is browned
both sides and just cooked through.
Serve fish with onion and lime.

SERVES 4
Per serving 16.1g fat; 1328kJ

lamb, spinach
and fetta stir-fry

2 tablespoons garlic-flavoured oil

1 medium brown onion (150g), sliced thinly

500g lamb fillets, sliced thinly

500g cherry tomatoes

200g baby spinach leaves

200g fetta cheese, crumbled

Heat wok or large frying pan, add oil; stir-fry onion and lamb, in batches, until browned and tender, remove from wok. **Stir-fry** tomatoes until soft. Return lamb mixture to wok with spinach; stir-fry until spinach is just wilted. Add fetta; stir-fry until just combined.

SERVES 4
Per serving 25.7g fat; 1672kJ

fettuccine with broccoli, **salami** and sun-dried tomatoes

500g fettuccine

120g thinly sliced salami

300g broccoli, chopped coarsely

600ml thickened light cream

²/₃ cup (100g) drained sun-dried tomatoes in oil, chopped coarsely

2 tablespoons finely grated parmesan cheese

Cook pasta in large saucepan of boiling water, uncovered, until just tender; drain. Cover pasta to keep warm.

Meanwhile, cut salami into thin strips; cook in medium heated non-stick frying pan, stirring, until crisp, drain on absorbent paper.

Boil, steam or microwave broccoli until tender; drain.

Bring cream to a boil in large saucepan, add salami, broccoli, tomato and parmesan, stir until hot. Add pasta to pan; mix gently.

SERVES 4

Per serving 27.5g fat; 3006kJ

22 salami pizza with
garlic pizza crusts

2 large frozen
pizza bases

1/4 cup (60ml)
tomato paste

1 clove garlic, crushed

2 tablespoons finely
chopped fresh
basil leaves

1 small brown onion
(80g), sliced thinly

50g sliced salami,
cut into thin strips

1 stick cabanossi
(125g), sliced thinly

1/2 cup (60g) seeded
black olives

1 cup (100g)
coarsely grated
mozzarella cheese

1 cup (125g)
coarsely grated
cheddar cheese

30g butter, softened

4 cloves garlic,
crushed, extra

Place pizza bases on oven trays, spread one
base with combined paste, garlic and basil.
Top with onion, salami, cabanossi and olives.
Sprinkle with half of the combined mozzarella
and cheddar. Bake in hot oven about
20 minutes or until crisp.

Meanwhile, spread remaining base with
combined butter and extra garlic; sprinkle with
remaining cheeses. Bake in hot oven about
15 minutes or until browned.

Sprinkle salami pizza with extra fresh basil
leaves, if desired.

SERVES 4
Per serving 41.4g fat; 3274kJ

satay **beef** skewers

¼ cup fresh coriander leaves

850g beef rump steak

½ cup (125ml) satay sauce

2 Lebanese cucumbers (260g)

2 green onions, sliced thinly

2 tablespoons sweet chilli sauce

Chop 2 tablespoons of the coriander. Cut beef into 2cm pieces; combine with chopped coriander and half of the satay sauce in large dish, cover; stand 10 minutes.

Using a vegetable peeler, slice cucumbers into thin strips. Combine cucumber in medium bowl with onion, remaining coriander and chilli sauce.

Thread undrained beef onto eight skewers. Char-grill (or grill or barbecue) skewers, until browned all over and cooked as desired. Serve skewers with remaining satay sauce and cucumber mixture.

SERVES 4
Per serving 13.8g fat; 1475kJ

24 beef and

vegetable stir-fry

750g beef rump steak, sliced thinly

1 tablespoon grated fresh ginger

2 tablespoons lemon juice

2 tablespoons honey

¼ cup (60ml) tomato sauce

2 tablespoons peanut oil

500g packet fresh stir-fry vegetables

2 tablespoons soy sauce

Combine beef in large bowl with half of the combined ginger, juice, honey and tomato sauce. **Heat** half of the oil in wok or large frying pan; stir-fry undrained beef mixture, in batches, until browned. Heat remaining oil in same wok; stir-fry vegetables until just tender. Return beef to wok with remaining tomato sauce mixture and soy sauce; stir-fry until sauce boils.

SERVES 4

Per serving 18.2g fat; 1801kJ

lamb cutlets with beetroot
and tzatziki

12 (780g) lamb cutlets

2 tablespoons
lemon juice

2 cloves garlic, crushed

2 tablespoons olive oil

900g baby beetroot

250g tub tzatziki dip

Combine lamb, juice,
garlic and oil in
large bowl.
Trim leaves from
beetroot; discard
leaves. Boil, steam or
microwave unpeeled
beetroot until tender,
drain; cool. Peel
beetroot, cut
into quarters.
Drain lamb from
marinade, discard
marinade. Char-grill
(or grill or barbecue)
lamb, until browned
both sides and
cooked as desired.
Serve lamb with
beetroot; top
with tzatziki.

SERVES 4
Per serving
25.2g fat; 1745kJ

chicken and pea risotto

1.25 litres (5 cups) chicken stock

60g butter

4 green onions, sliced thinly

1 clove garlic, crushed

2 teaspoons fresh thyme leaves

1¹/₂ cups (300g) arborio rice

1¹/₂ cups (185g) frozen peas

2 cups (340g) coarsely chopped cooked chicken

1 cup (80g) finely grated parmesan cheese

Bring stock to a boil in medium saucepan, reduce to a simmer.

Melt butter in large saucepan; cook onion, garlic and thyme, stirring, until onion is soft. Add rice; cook, stirring, about 1 minute or until rice is coated with butter mixture. Add ¹/₂ cup (125ml) of the simmering stock; stir rice mixture constantly over medium heat until all liquid is absorbed.

Continue adding simmering stock, ¹/₂ cup (125ml) at a time, stirring until absorbed between additions. Total cooking time will be about 25 minutes or until rice is creamy and just tender.

Meanwhile, pour boiling water over peas; stand 2 minutes, drain.

Stir peas and chicken into risotto, stir until hot. Remove from heat, stir in cheese.

SERVES 4
Per serving 26.6g fat; 2772kJ

sesame fish with soy and chilli sauce

4 (800g) firm white fish fillets
plain flour
1 egg, beaten lightly
1 cup (150g) sesame seeds
vegetable oil, for shallow-frying

soy and chilli sauce
2 green onions, sliced thinly
½ cup (125ml) light soy sauce
1 tablespoon sweet chilli sauce

Toss fish in flour, shake off excess. Dip fish in egg, then coat in sesame seeds. Heat oil in large frying pan; shallow-fry fish until browned both sides and cooked through, drain on absorbent paper. Serve fish with Soy and Chilli Sauce.
Soy and Chilli Sauce Combine ingredients in small bowl.

SERVES 4
Per serving 55.4g fat; 2245kJ

garlic thyme barbecued
spatchcocks

4 x 500g spatchcocks

1 medium lime (80g)

¼ cup (60ml) olive oil

1 tablespoon finely chopped fresh thyme

1 tablespoon cracked black pepper

2 cloves garlic, crushed

Place spatchcocks, breast-side down, on board. Cut along both sides of backbone, discard bones. Rinse spatchcocks, pat dry with absorbent paper.

Grate rind of lime finely, squeeze juice from lime. Combine oil, thyme, pepper, garlic, rind and juice in large dish; add spatchcocks, turn to coat in oil mixture. Cover; stand 10 minutes.

Drain spatchcocks from marinade, reserve marinade. Barbecue (or grill or char-grill) spatchcocks, until browned both sides and cooked through, brushing with reserved marinade several times during cooking. Serve with barbecued eggplant and zucchini, if desired.

SERVES 4
Per serving 37.4g fat; 2370kJ

cajun-style
steak sandwiches

2 tablespoons Cajun seasoning

2 tablespoons olive oil

8 (800g) beef minute steaks

1 large brown onion (200g), sliced thinly

1/2 small red capsicum (75g), sliced thinly

1/2 small green capsicum (75g), sliced thinly

1/2 small yellow capsicum (75g), sliced thinly

1/2 cup (125ml) water

8 x 2cm-thick slices bread

Rub combined seasoning and half of the oil over beef.

Heat remaining oil in large frying pan; cook onion, capsicum strips and the water, covered, until capsicum is soft, stirring occasionally. Remove from pan, cover to keep warm.

Cook beef, in batches, in same pan, until browned both sides and cooked as desired.

Meanwhile, toast bread. Top four slices of toast with beef and capsicum mixture, then remaining toast slices.

SERVES 4
Per serving 21.3g fat; 2267kJ

¼ *cup (65g) red curry paste*

1⅔ *cups (400ml) coconut milk*

½ *cup (125ml) water*

250g green beans, halved

750g firm white fish fillets, sliced thickly

¼ *cup finely chopped fresh coriander leaves*

Cook paste in large, heated non-stick frying pan, stirring, until fragrant. **Add** coconut milk and the water; bring to a boil. Add beans; simmer, covered, 2 minutes. Add fish; simmer, covered, until fish is just cooked. Stir in coriander.

SERVES 4
Per serving 30g fat; 1939kJ

perfect partners

The meal is made, but now you need an accompaniment to it that's quick and complementary. Try these delicious side-serves on for size.

fruit and almond couscous

2 cups (400g) couscous

2 cups (500ml) boiling chicken stock

40g butter

¼ cup (35g) dried currants

¼ cup (35g) finely chopped dried apricots

¼ cup (35g) slivered almonds

1 tablespoon finely chopped fresh coriander leaves

Place couscous in medium heatproof bowl; add stock and butter. Gently toss couscous, using a fork, until all the liquid is absorbed. Add remaining ingredients, mix gently.

SERVES 4
Per serving 13.8g fat; 2238kJ

italian mashed potato

4 medium potatoes (800g), chopped coarsely

40g butter

¼ cup (60ml) milk

1 teaspoon sugar

¼ cup (20g) finely grated parmesan cheese

¼ cup (30g) seeded black olives, sliced thinly

1 tablespoon finely chopped fresh basil leaves

Boil, steam or microwave potato until tender; drain, mash well. Add butter, milk and sugar; beat until butter is melted. Stir in remaining ingredients.

SERVES 4
Per serving 10.7g fat; 1036kJ

indian rice

2 teaspoons peanut oil

1 medium brown onion (150g), chopped finely

1 clove garlic, crushed

½ teaspoon ground turmeric

1 teaspoon ground coriander

1 teaspoon ground cumin

1 teaspoon garam masala

1½ cups (300g) white long-grain rice

3 cups (750ml) chicken stock

Heat oil in medium heavy-base saucepan; cook onion and garlic, stirring, until onion is soft. Add spices; cook, stirring, until fragrant. Stir in rice, then stock; bring to a boil. Simmer, covered, 12 minutes. Remove from heat; stand, covered, 10 minutes.

SERVES 4
Per serving 3.8g fat; 1350kJ

From top: fruit and almond couscous; italian mashed potato; indian rice

cheese tortellini salad with
mustard mayonnaise

250g fresh cheese tortellini

250g asparagus, cut into 4cm pieces

200g baby green beans, trimmed

1 small red capsicum (150g), sliced thickly

1 small green capsicum (150g), sliced thickly

100g button mushrooms, quartered

4 green onions, cut into 4cm pieces

mustard mayonnaise

2 egg yolks

1 tablespoon lemon juice

3/4 cup (180ml) olive oil

1 tablespoon seeded mustard

1 clove garlic, crushed

2 teaspoons water

Cook pasta in large saucepan of boiling water, uncovered, until just tender; drain, cool.
Boil, steam or microwave asparagus and beans, separately, until just tender, rinse under cold water; drain.
Combine pasta and vegetables in large bowl; drizzle with Mustard Mayonnaise.
Mustard Mayonnaise Blend or process egg yolks and juice until pale and thick. With motor operating, gradually pour in oil in a thin stream; blend until thick. Stir in mustard, garlic and the water.

SERVES 4
Per serving 48.6g fat; 2231kJ

vegetarian tagine

1 tablespoon olive oil

1 medium brown onion (150g), chopped coarsely

1 clove garlic, crushed

1½ tablespoons ground cumin

1 tablespoon ground coriander

2 teaspoons caraway seeds

2 medium eggplants (600g), chopped coarsely

1 large zucchini (150g), chopped coarsely

4 medium tomatoes (760g), chopped coarsely

300g can chickpeas, rinsed, drained

1 tablespoon lemon juice

1 cup (250ml) vegetable stock

⅓ cup coarsely chopped fresh coriander leaves

Heat oil in large saucepan; cook onion, garlic, spices, seeds and eggplant, stirring, until onion is soft. Add zucchini, tomato and chickpeas; cook, stirring, about 5 minutes or until vegetables are just tender. Stir in juice and stock; cook, stirring, until mixture boils and thickens.

Just before serving, stir in coriander. Serve vegetarian tagine with couscous, if desired.

SERVES 4
Per serving 7.5g fat; 763kJ

minute steaks with

coriander butter

4 (800g) beef minute steaks

coriander butter

40g butter, softened

1 tablespoon finely chopped fresh coriander leaves

1 teaspoon mild curry powder

1 tablespoon lime juice

1 clove garlic, crushed

Char-grill (or grill or barbecue) beef, until browned both sides and cooked as desired. Top beef with thinly sliced Coriander Butter.
Coriander Butter Combine ingredients in small bowl. Spoon mixture onto sheet of foil, shape into a log. Roll up firmly, freeze about 10 minutes or until firm.

SERVES 4
Per serving 17.9g fat; 1385kJ

38 blackened **fish** with

lemon butter

4 *(800g) firm white fish cutlets*

20g butter, melted

1 teaspoon garlic salt

2 teaspoons cracked black pepper

½ teaspoon sweet paprika

1½ teaspoons dried thyme leaves

lemon butter

60g butter, melted

1 green onion, sliced thinly

1 tablespoon lemon juice

Brush both sides of fish with butter, sprinkle evenly with combined remaining ingredients. **Barbecue** (or grill or char-grill) fish, until browned both sides and just cooked through. Serve fish drizzled with Lemon Butter. **Lemon Butter** Combine ingredients in small bowl.

SERVES 4
Per serving 21g fat; 1500kJ

easy niçoise-style salad 39

125g green beans

2 x 425g cans tuna, drained

410g can Tiny Taters, drained, quartered

250g cherry tomatoes, halved

1 cup (120g) seeded black olives

1 large red oak leaf lettuce

dressing

1/3 cup (80ml) olive oil

1 tablespoon white wine vinegar

2 teaspoons seeded mustard

1 teaspoon sugar

1 clove garlic, crushed

Place beans in large heatproof bowl, cover with boiling water, stand 5 minutes; drain. Rinse beans under cold water; drain well.

Break tuna into large chunks. Combine beans and tuna with remaining ingredients in large bowl; drizzle with Dressing.

Dressing Combine ingredients in jar; shake well.

SERVES 4
Per serving 23.1g fat; 1904kJ

ricotta ravioli with pumpkin sauce

1/4 cup (60ml) olive oil

1 small brown onion (80g), chopped finely

1 clove garlic, crushed

600g butternut pumpkin, sliced thinly

1 1/2 cups (375ml) chicken stock

1/2 teaspoon ground nutmeg

1/2 cup (125ml) thickened light cream

600g fresh ricotta ravioli

1/3 cup (50g) pine nuts, toasted

2 tablespoons coarsely chopped fresh chives

Heat half of the oil in large frying pan; cook onion and garlic, stirring, until onion is soft. Remove from pan.
Heat remaining oil in same pan; cook pumpkin until browned both sides. Return onion to pan with stock and nutmeg. Cook, stirring, until liquid is absorbed and pumpkin mashed; stir in cream.
Meanwhile, cook pasta in large saucepan of boiling water, uncovered, until tender; drain.
Serve pasta with pumpkin sauce, top with nuts and chives.

SERVES 4
Per serving 29.5g fat; 1883kJ

chicken salad with
sesame dressing

1 large cooked
chicken

2 medium
carrots (240g)

1 small Chinese
cabbage (400g),
chopped coarsely

6 green onions,
sliced thickly

1 cup (80g)
bean sprouts

1/4 cup firmly packed
fresh coriander leaves

sesame dressing

2 cloves garlic,
crushed

1/2 teaspoon
sesame oil

2 tablespoons
peanut oil

1 tablespoon
soy sauce

1 tablespoon
lemon juice

1 teaspoon sugar

1 tablespoon white
wine vinegar

Cut chicken into eight pieces. Using a
vegetable peeler, slice carrots into thin strips.
Combine carrot, cabbage, onion, sprouts
and coriander on serving plates; top with
chicken. Drizzle salad and chicken with
Sesame Dressing.

Sesame Dressing Combine ingredients
in screw-top jar; shake well.

SERVES 4
Per serving 17.6g fat; 1264kJ

tandoori lamb with grilled limes

8 (1.4kg) lamb chump chops, trimmed

1 clove garlic, crushed

¼ cup (65g) tandoori paste

2 medium limes (160g), sliced thickly

½ cup (175g) mango chutney

200ml yogurt

2 tablespoons finely chopped fresh coriander leaves

Combine lamb, garlic and paste in large bowl. Cover; refrigerate 10 minutes. **Char-grill** (or grill or barbecue) lamb and limes, until lamb is browned both sides and cooked as desired and limes are browned both sides. **Serve** lamb with lime slices, mango chutney and combined yogurt and coriander.

SERVES 4
Per serving
34.2g fat; 2738kJ

44 dry malaysian
chicken curry

1/4 cup (60ml) vegetable oil

8 (1.3kg) chicken thigh cutlets

4 medium brown onions
(600g), sliced thinly

2 tablespoons grated
fresh ginger

1 cinnamon stick

2 teaspoons chilli powder

2 teaspoons ground cumin

2 teaspoons ground coriander

2 tablespoons lime juice

Heat half of the oil in large frying pan; cook chicken, in batches, until browned all over, drain on absorbent paper.
Heat remaining oil in same pan; cook onion, ginger, cinnamon, chilli and spices, stirring, until onion is soft.
Return chicken to pan with juice; cook, covered, about 15 minutes or until chicken is cooked through. Remove and discard cinnamon.

SERVES 4
Per serving 30.9g fat; 2089kJ

creamy mushroom and
bacon pasta sauce

250g fusilli pasta

1 tablespoon olive oil

1 medium brown onion
(150g), chopped finely

4 bacon rashers,
sliced thinly

2 tablespoons
pine nuts

250g button
mushrooms,
sliced thinly

½ cup (125ml)
sour cream

1 egg, beaten lightly

¼ cup (20g) finely
grated parmesan
cheese

¼ cup finely chopped
fresh parsley

Cook pasta in large saucepan of boiling water,
uncovered, until just tender; drain.
Meanwhile, heat oil in large frying pan; cook
onion, bacon and pine nuts, stirring, until onion
is soft. Add mushrooms; cook, stirring, until
mushrooms are soft. Stir in remaining
ingredients; stir over low heat until heated
through. Serve sauce over pasta.

SERVES 4
Per serving 28.1g fat; 2225kJ

asian-style chicken
noodle soup

1 tablespoon peanut oil

500g chicken thigh fillets, sliced thinly

2 teaspoons grated fresh ginger

100g shiitake mushrooms, sliced thinly

1.5 litres (6 cups) chicken stock

2 cups (500ml) water

1 tablespoon soy sauce

1/2 teaspoon sesame oil

1/4 cup (35g) cornflour

1/4 cup (60ml) water, extra

85g packet instant noodles

130g can corn kernels, drained

130g can creamed corn

6 green onions, chopped finely

Heat peanut oil in large saucepan; cook chicken, in batches, until browned lightly.
Add ginger and mushrooms; cook, stirring, until fragrant. Add stock, the water, sauce and sesame oil.
Stir in blended cornflour and extra water; cook, stirring, until soup boils and thickens. Break noodles in half, add to soup with both types of corn and onion. Simmer, uncovered, about 2 minutes or until noodles are tender.

SERVES 4
Per serving 17.5g fat; 1607kJ

chicken with mushroom
paprika sauce

1 tablespoon olive oil

4 (680g) single
chicken breast fillets

1 medium brown onion
(150g), sliced thinly

80g button mushrooms,
sliced thickly

1/2 teaspoon
sweet paprika

1/2 cup (125ml) light
sour cream

1 tablespoon
lemon juice

1/3 cup (80ml)
chicken stock

2 tablespoons finely
chopped dill pickles

1 tablespoon finely
chopped fresh
coriander leaves

Heat oil in large frying pan; cook chicken,
until browned both sides and cooked through.
Remove chicken from pan, cover to keep warm.
Cook onion in same pan, stirring, until soft.
Add mushrooms and paprika; cook, stirring,
until mushrooms are soft. Add cream, juice,
stock and pickles, stir until hot (do not boil).
Stir in coriander.
Serve chicken with sauce.

SERVES 4
Per serving 20.6g fat; 1511kJ

chicken sausages with
leek and mash

4 medium potatoes (800g), chopped coarsely

⅓ cup (80ml) sour cream

1 tablespoon seeded mustard

12 (750g) chicken sausages

2 medium leeks (700g), sliced thinly

1 tablespoon brown sugar

Boil, steam or microwave potato until tender; drain, mash. Add sour cream and mustard, beat until combined.

Meanwhile, cook sausages in large heated non-stick frying pan, until browned all over and cooked through. Remove sausages from pan; cover to keep warm.

Cook leek in same pan, stirring, until browned. Add sugar, stir until caramelised. Serve sausages with leek and mashed potato.

SERVES 4
Per serving 50.8g fat; 3053kJ

50 quick saltimbocca

2 tablespoons olive oil

24 fresh sage laves

200g thinly sliced leg ham, halved

60g butter

8 (720g) veal schnitzels

½ cup (125ml) dry red wine

Heat oil in large frying pan, add sage; cook until crisp, remove from pan. Add ham to same pan; cook, stirring, until crisp. Remove from pan.
Heat half of the butter in same pan; cook veal, in batches, until browned both sides and just tender, remove from pan, cover to keep warm.
Add wine to pan; simmer, uncovered, until reduced by a third, stir in remaining butter.
Serve veal topped with ham and sage; drizzle with sauce.

SERVES 4
Per serving 24.4g fat; 2033kJ

mexican

chicken burgers

2 medium avocados (500g), mashed

¹⁄₄ cup finely chopped fresh coriander leaves

4 (680g) single chicken breast fillets

35g packet taco seasoning mix

4 burger buns

¹⁄₃ cup (80ml) mild tomato salsa

Combine avocado and coriander in medium bowl.
Coat chicken in taco seasoning mix. Char-grill (or grill or barbecue) chicken, until browned both sides and cooked through. Slice chicken thickly.
Split buns in half; grill, cut-side up, until lightly toasted. Place chicken on base of buns, top with avocado mixture and salsa; replace top of buns.

SERVES 4
Per serving
32.3g fat; 2468kJ

broccoli and potato in

spicy coriander sauce

2 tablespoons vegetable oil

1 tablespoon cumin seeds

3 teaspoons ground coriander

1/2 teaspoon sweet paprika

500g broccoli, chopped coarsely

4 medium potatoes (800g), chopped coarsely

4 medium tomatoes (760g), peeled

1/4 cup (60g) tomato paste

1/2 cup (125ml) water

1/4 cup coarsely chopped fresh coriander leaves

Heat oil in large frying pan; cook seeds, ground coriander and paprika, stirring, over medium heat 1 minute. Add broccoli and potato; cook, stirring, over medium heat 1 minute.

Blend or process tomatoes, paste and the water until smooth; add to broccoli mixture.

Bring to a boil; simmer gently, uncovered, stirring occasionally, about 20 minutes or until potato is tender.

Stir in fresh coriander just before serving.

SERVES 4
Per serving 10.6g fat; 1069kJ

54 butter bean and
vegetable salad

4 medium tomatoes
(760g), chopped
coarsely

1 large red onion
(300g), sliced thinly

6 green onions,
sliced thinly

3 x 300g cans butter
beans, rinsed, drained

1 large red capsicum
(350g), chopped
coarsely

2 Lebanese
cucumbers (260g),
seeded, sliced thickly

200g fetta cheese,
crumbled

1/3 cup (80ml)
lemon juice

2 tablespoons olive oil

1 clove garlic, crushed

1 teaspoon sugar

1/2 teaspoon
sweet paprika

Combine tomato,
onions, beans,
capsicum, cucumber
and cheese in large
bowl; gently toss with
combined remaining
ingredients just
before serving.

SERVES 4
Per serving
21.6g fat; 1417kJ

veal with

mustard sauce

1 tablespoon
vegetable oil

4 (360g) veal
schnitzels

20g butter

3 green onions,
chopped finely

2 tablespoons
French mustard

300ml cream

2 tablespoons finely
chopped fresh chives

Heat oil in large frying pan; cook veal until
browned both sides and cooked as desired.
Remove veal from pan; cover to keep warm.
Melt butter in same pan; cook onion, stirring,
until soft. Add mustard, cream and half of the
chives; simmer, uncovered, until sauce has
thickened slightly. Serve sauce over veal,
sprinkle with remaining chives.

SERVES 4
Per serving 44.5g fat; 2164kJ

8 (1.3kg) chicken thigh cutlets

1/3 cup (80ml) vegetable oil

1/3 cup (80ml) lime juice

2 cloves garlic, crushed

1 tablespoon honey

1 teaspoon mixed dried herbs

1 teaspoon sweet paprika

1/2 teaspoon chilli powder

1/2 teaspoon ground allspice

Combine chicken with remaining ingredients in large bowl, cover; refrigerate 10 minutes.
Drain chicken from marinade; reserve marinade. Grill (or char-grill or barbecue) chicken, until browned both sides and cooked through.
Meanwhile, bring reserved marinade to a boil in small saucepan; simmer, uncovered, 2 minutes. Drizzle marinade mixture over chicken.

SERVES 4
Per serving 35.1g fat; 2127kJ

and beans

1 tablespoon olive oil

800g beef chipolata sausages

2 large brown onions (400g), sliced thinly

2 cloves garlic, crushed

6 large egg tomatoes (540g)

400g can cannellini beans, rinsed, drained

1 tablespoon finely chopped fresh thyme

Heat oil in large frying pan; cook sausages, onion and garlic, in batches, until sausages are browned and cooked through.

Cut tomatoes into wedges; cook in same pan with beans until just hot.

Return sausage mixture to pan; cook, tossing to combine ingredients.

Serve sausage mixture sprinkled with thyme.

SERVES 4
Per serving
60.7g fat; 3137kJ

quick minestrone

1 tablespoon olive oil

1 medium carrot (120g), chopped coarsely

1 trimmed stick celery (75g),
chopped coarsely

1 medium leek (350g), chopped coarsely

3 bacon rashers, chopped coarsely

1 medium potato (200g), chopped coarsely

2 x 400g cans tomatoes

3 cups (750ml) vegetable stock

1.25 litres (5 cups) water

150g small pasta shapes

300g can butter beans, rinsed, drained

1 cup (110g) chopped frozen green beans

Heat oil in large saucepan; cook carrot, celery, leek, bacon and potato, stirring, until leek is soft.

Stir in undrained crushed tomatoes, stock and the water. Bring to a boil, add pasta; simmer, uncovered, about 10 minutes or until pasta is tender. Add both beans; simmer, uncovered, until hot.

SERVES 4
Per serving 9g fat; 1419kJ

glossary

arborio rice small, round-grained white rice, well-suited to absorb a large amount of cooking liquid.

bacon rashers also known as slices of bacon; made from pork side, cured and smoked. Streaky bacon is the fatty end of a bacon rasher (slice), without the lean (eye) meat.

bean sprouts also known as bean shoots; tender new growths of assorted beans and seeds germinated for consumption as sprouts.

beetroot also known as beets.

bread

pide: also known as Turkish bread; comes in long flat loaves and small rounds. Made from wheat flour then sprinkled with sesame or black onion seeds.

pitta: Lebanese wheat-flour bread.

cabanossi a ready-to-eat sausage; also known as cabana.

cajun seasoning blend of ground spices that can include paprika, basil, onion, fennel, thyme, cayenne and tarragon.

capsicum also known as bell pepper or, simply, pepper.

cheese

fetta: Greek in origin; crumbly-textured goat- or sheep-milk cheese with sharp, salty taste.

ricotta: fresh, unripened cheese made from whey.

chicken, minced ground chicken.

chickpeas also called garbanzos or channa; an irregularly round, sandy-coloured legume used extensively in Mediterranean and Middle Eastern cooking.

chipolatas tiny sausages.

coconut

cream: the first pressing from grated mature coconut flesh; available in cans and cartons.

milk: the second pressing (less rich) from grated mature coconut flesh; available in cans and cartons, and in a reduced-fat form.

couscous a fine, grain-like cereal product made from semolina.

cream

fresh: also known as pure cream and pouring cream; has minimum fat content 35% and no additives (like commercially thickened cream).

light sour: has minimum fat content 18%; cream specifically cultured to produce a characteristic tart flavour. Thinner than normal sour cream so should not be substituted in cooking because the consistency will affect recipe results.

sour: a thick, commercially cultured soured cream (minimum fat content 35%); good for dips, toppings and baked cheesecakes.

thickened light: has minimum fat content 35%; a whipping cream containing a thickener.

eggplant also known as aubergine.

flour, plain an all-purpose flour made from wheat.

garam masala a spice blend; includes cardamom, cloves, cinnamon, fennel, coriander and cumin, roasted and ground together. Black pepper and chilli can be added for a hotter version.

lamb, minced ground lamb.

mushrooms

button: small, cultivated white mushrooms having a delicate, subtle flavour.

flat: large, soft, flat mushrooms with a rich earthy flavour; some greengrocers may call them field mushrooms.

shiitake: used mainly in Chinese and Japanese cooking.

swiss brown: light to dark brown mushrooms with full-bodied flavour. Button or cup mushrooms can be substituted for Swiss brown mushrooms.

mustard seeds, black also known as brown mustard seeds; more pungent than the white (or yellow) seeds used in most mustards.

oil

peanut: made from ground peanuts; most commonly used oil in Asian cooking. Has high smoke point.

sesame: made from roasted, crushed white sesame seeds; an aromatic, golden-coloured oil with a nutty flavour. Should not be used to fry food; add towards end of cooking time to add flavour.

onion, green also known as scallion or, incorrectly, shallot; an onion picked before the bulb has formed, having a long, bright green, edible stalk.

salami highly spiced, cured, air-dried sausage, usually made with a mix of beef and pork.

snake beans long (about 40cm), thin, round green beans; Asian in origin.

snow peas also known as mange tout ("eat all").

spatchcock a small chicken (poussin), no more than six weeks old, weighing a maximum 500g.

spinach also known as English spinach and, incorrectly, silverbeet.

stock 1 cup (250ml) stock is the equivalent of 1 cup (250ml) water plus 1 crumbled stock cube (or 1 teaspoon stock powder).

sugar we used coarse, granulated table sugar, also known as crystal sugar, unless otherwise specified.

brown: soft, finely granulated sugar retaining molasses for its characteristic colour and flavour.

tagine a Moroccan stew often served with couscous.

tiny taters canned baby potatoes available from supermarkets.

tortillas thin, round, unleavened bread originating in Mexico; available made from wheat-flour or corn (maizemeal).

tzatziki cucumber and garlic dip.

vinegar

balsamic: authentic only from province of Modena, Italy; made from wine of white Trebbiano grapes, aged in antique wooden casks.

cider: made from fermented apples.

white wine: made from fermented white wine.

zucchini also known as courgette.

index

facts and figures 63

These conversions are approximate only, but the difference between an exact and the approximate conversion of various liquid and dry measures is minimal and will not affect your cooking results.

Measuring equipment

The difference between one country's measuring cups and another's is, at most, within a 2 or 3 teaspoon variance. (For the record, 1 Australian metric measuring cup holds approximately 250ml.) The most accurate way of measuring dry ingredients is to weigh them. For liquids, use a clear glass or plastic jug having metric markings.

Note: NZ, Canada, USA and UK all use 15ml tablespoons. Australian tablespoons measure 20ml.
All cup and spoon measurements are level.

How to measure

When using graduated measuring cups, shake dry ingredients loosely into the appropriate cup. Do not tap the cup on a bench or tightly pack the ingredients unless directed to do so. Level the top of measuring cups and measuring spoons with a knife. When measuring liquids, place a clear glass or plastic jug, having metric markings, on a flat surface to check accuracy at eye level.

Dry Measures

metric	imperial
15g	1/2oz
30g	1oz
60g	2oz
90g	3oz
125g	4oz (1/4lb)
155g	5oz
185g	6oz
220g	7oz
250g	8oz (1/2lb)
280g	9oz
315g	10oz
345g	11oz
375g	12oz (3/4lb)
410g	13oz
440g	14oz
470g	15oz
500g	16oz (1lb)
750g	24oz (1 1/2lb)
1kg	32oz (2lb)

We use large eggs having an average weight of 60g.

Liquid Measures

metric	imperial
30ml	1 fluid oz
60ml	2 fluid oz
100ml	3 fluid oz
125ml	4 fluid oz
150ml	5 fluid oz (1/4 pint/1 gill)
190ml	6 fluid oz
250ml (1cup)	8 fluid oz
300ml	10 fluid oz (1/2 pint)
500ml	16 fluid oz
600ml	20 fluid oz (1 pint)
1000ml (1litre)	1 3/4 pints

Helpful Measures

metric	imperial
3mm	1/8in
6mm	1/4in
1cm	1/2in
2cm	3/4in
2.5cm	1in
6cm	2 1/2in
8cm	3in
20cm	8in
23cm	9in
25cm	10in
30cm	12in (1ft)

Oven Temperatures

These oven temperatures are only a guide.
Always check the manufacturer's manual.

	°C (Celsius)	°F (Fahrenheit)	Gas Mark
Very slow	120	250	1
Slow	150	300	2
Moderately slow	160	325	3
Moderate	180 –190	350 – 375	4
Moderately hot	200 – 210	400 – 425	5
Hot	220 – 230	450 – 475	6
Very hot	240 – 250	500 – 525	7

at your fingertips

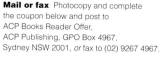

These elegant slipcovers store up to 10 mini books and make the books instantly accessible.

And the metric measuring cups and spoons make following our recipes a piece of cake.

Book Holder
Australia: $13.10 (incl. GST).
Elsewhere: $A21.95.

Metric Measuring Set
Australia: $6.50 (incl. GST).
New Zealand: $A8.00.
Elsewhere: $A9.95.
Prices include postage and handling. This offer is available in all countries.

Photocopy and complete coupon below

Mail or fax Photocopy and complete the coupon below and post to ACP Books Reader Offer, ACP Publishing, GPO Box 4967, Sydney NSW 2001, *or* fax to (02) 9267 4967.

Phone Have your credit card details ready, then phone 136 116 (Mon-Fri, 8.00am-6.00pm; Sat, 8.00am-6.00pm).

Australian residents
We accept the credit cards listed on the coupon, money orders and cheques.
Overseas residents We accept the credit cards listed on the coupon, drafts in $A drawn on an Australian bank, and also British, New Zealand and U.S. cheques in the currency of the country of issue. Credit card charges are at the exchange rate current at the time of payment.

- -

☐ Book Holder   ☐ Metric Measuring Set

Please indicate number(s) required.

Mr/Mrs/Ms _____

Address _____

_____

Postcode _____ Country _____

Ph: Business hours ( ) _____

I enclose my cheque/money order for $ _____ payable to ACP Publishing.

OR: please charge $ _____ to my   ☐ Bankcard   ☐ Mastercard

☐ Visa   ☐ American Express   ☐ Diners Club

Expiry date ____ /____

Card number

Cardholder's signature _____

Please allow up to 30 days delivery within Australia.
Allow up to 6 weeks for overseas deliveries.
Both offers expire 31/12/03. HRTMM02

Food editor Pamela Clark
Associate food editor Karen Hammial
Assistant food editor Kathy McGarry
Assistant recipe editor Elizabeth Hooper
ACP BOOKS STAFF

Editorial director Susan Tomnay
Creative director Hieu Nguyen
Senior editor Julie Collard
Concept design Jackie Richards
Designer Mary Keep
Publishing manager (sales) Jennifer McDonald
Publishing manager (rights & new titles) Jane Hazell
Assistant brand manager Donna Gianniotis
Pre-press by Harry Palmer
Production manager Carol Currie

Publisher Sue Wannan
Group publisher Jill Baker
Chief executive officer John Alexander

Produced by ACP Books, Sydney.
Printing by Dai Nippon Printing in Hong Kong.
Published by ACP Publishing Pty Limited, 54 Park St, Sydney; GPO Box 4088, Sydney, NSW 1028. Ph: (02) 9282 8618 Fax: (02) 9267 9438.
acpbooks@acp.com.au
www.acpbooks.com.au
To order books phone 136 116.
Send recipe enquiries to
Recipeenquiries@acp.com.au

Australia Distributed by Network Services, GPO Box 4088, Sydney, NSW 1028. Ph: (02) 9282 8777 Fax: (02) 9264 3278.
United Kingdom Distributed by Australian Consolidated Press (UK), Moulton Park Business Centre, Red House Road, Moulton Park, Northampton, NN3 6AQ. Ph: (01604) 497 531 Fax: (01604) 497 533 acpukltd@aol.com
Canada Distributed by Whitecap Books Ltd, 351 Lynn Ave, North Vancouver, BC, V7J 2C4, Ph: (604) 980 9852.
New Zealand Distributed by Netlink Distribution Company, Level 4, 23 Hargreaves St, College Hill, Auckland 1, Ph: (9) 302 7616.
South Africa Distributed by: PSD Promotions (Pty) Ltd, PO Box 1175, Isando 1600, SA, Ph: (011) 392 6065.

Clark, Pamela.
30-Minute Meals
Includes index.
ISBN 1 86396 207 7

1. Cookery. 2. Quick and easy cookery.
II. Title: Australian Women's Weekly.
(Series: Australian Women's Weekly mini series).
(Series: Australian Women's Weekly make it tonight).

641.555

© ACP Publishing Pty Limited 2000
ABN 18 053 273 546
This publication is copyright. No part of it may be reproduced or transmitted in any form without the written permission of the publishers.
First published 2000. Reprinted 2002.
Cover: Thai red curry fish, page 31.
Stylist Wendy Berecry
Photographer Ashley Mackevicius
Back cover: Ricotta ravioli with pumpkin sauce, page 40.

The publishers would like to thank Empire Homewares, Made in Japan and Orson & Blake Collectables for props used in photography.